D0753620

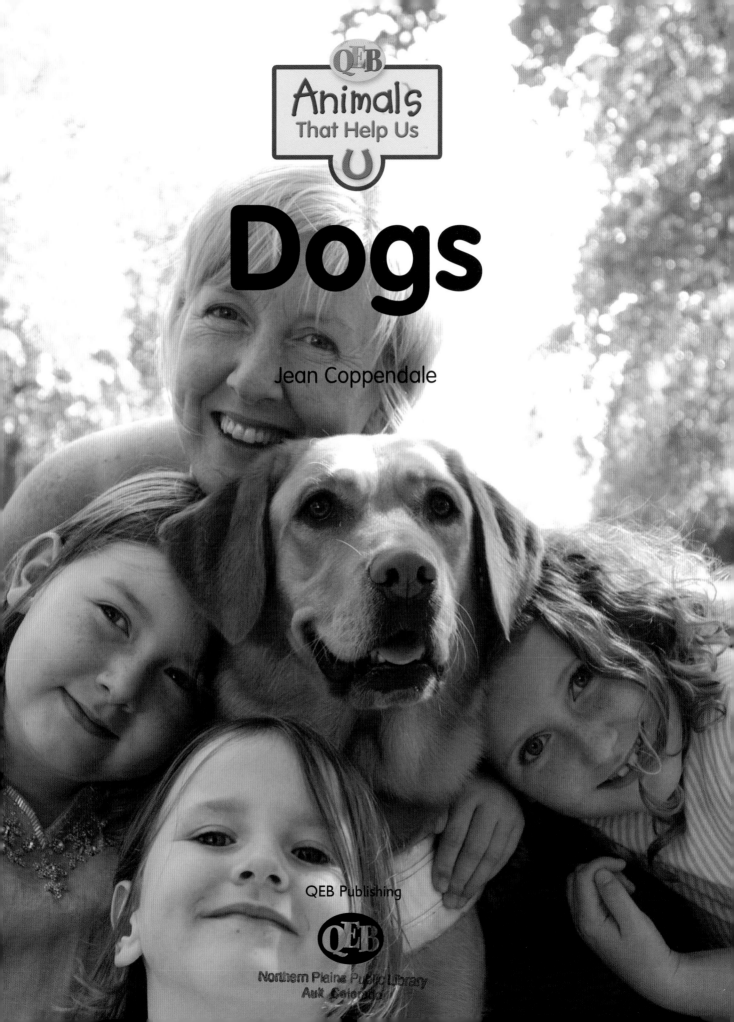

Animals That Help Us

Dogs

Jean Coppendale

QEB Publishing

QEB

Words in **bold** can be found in the Glossary on page 23.

Copyright © QEB Publishing, Inc. 2007

First published in the United States by
QEB Publishing, Inc.
23062 La Cadena Drive
Laguna Hills, CA 92653

www.qeb-publishing.com

Library of Congress Control Number: 2006038431

ISBN 978-1-59566-365-8

Written by Jean Coppendale
Designed by Melissa Alaverdy
Editor Paul Manning

Publisher Steve Evans
Creative Director Zeta Davies
Senior Editor Hannah Ray

Contents

How dogs help us

Dogs help us in many different ways. They help farmers look after sheep and **cattle**. They work with the police to keep us safe and help find people who are lost. Some dogs are trained to help people with **physical disabilities**, and pet dogs give us love and friendship.

Working dogs are loyal and often become very close to their owners.

With the right care
and lots of love,
a dog will be your
friend for life.

Dogs on the farm

For hundreds of years, dogs have worked on farms, helping farmers to look after their animals. Sheepdogs are used to round up sheep on the hills and in the fields. When all the sheep are together, the dogs will guide them back to the farm or into another field.

These sheepdogs are working as a team to keep the sheep under control.

Some **breeds** are better at doing certain jobs. This dog is good at working with cattle.

Tracking dogs

Dogs have a very strong sense of smell. Police dogs are trained to use their sense of smell to track down **criminals** and missing people.

Police officers who work with dogs are called dog handlers.

Before they do this, tracking dogs must first pick up the **scent** by sniffing something that belongs to the person, such as a handkerchief or a piece of clothing.

A tracking dog will follow the scent trail through the countryside, over fields, and through woods— wherever it may lead.

Specially trained dogs are often used at airports, train stations, and other public places to sniff out anything dangerous or **illegal**. When a sniffer dog smells something it has been trained to search for, it will scratch at the ground or bark until its handler comes to see what it has found.

A sniffer dog and its handler both crouch down to search for stolen goods hidden underneath a car.

A police officer and a sniffer dog at a station in London, in the United Kingdom.

Rescue dogs

If a building collapses in an accident or earthquake, dogs are used to find survivors who may be trapped underneath the rubble. The dogs try to pick up the scent of trapped people. They also use their excellent hearing to listen for anyone calling out. Then they bark to alert the rescue workers.

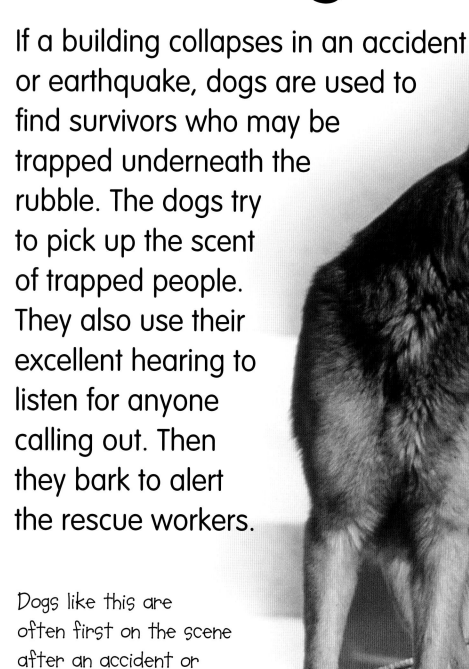

Dogs like this are often first on the scene after an accident or **natural disaster**.

Dogs are also trained to rescue climbers and hikers who are lost or injured in the mountains. This dog's special jacket helps it to be seen in bad weather.

Snow dogs

Huskies are dogs that live in very cold countries and help people by **herding** reindeer and pulling sleds. One husky is strong enough to pull a small sled on its own. On long journeys, teams of huskies take turns pulling sleds across the ice. Sometimes huskies will travel for several days through snow and icy winds.

This husky is wearing special boots to protect its paws from ice and cold.

Using a sled pulled by a team of huskies can be a good, fast way to travel from place to place in bad weather conditions.

Guide dogs

Guide dogs are specially trained to work with people who are blind or **partially sighted**. Guide dogs help these people with their daily lives. The dogs take their owners everywhere—to and from work, to the store, and to visit friends. They are also trained to help their owners get on and off buses and trains and to cross busy roads.

Only dogs that are gentle and enjoy being with people are chosen to be guide dogs.

Guide dogs must start their training at an early age to learn all the skills they will need.

Hearing dogs

Hearing dogs are special helpers for people who are deaf or who have hearing problems. When the dog hears the doorbell or some other noise, it will touch its owner gently with its paw to tell them that something is happening. Hearing dogs can also be trained to perform different signs for different noises.

As well as practical help, hearing dogs give their owners friendship, love, and enjoyment.

HEARING DOG FOR DEAF PEOPLE

Hearing Dogs for Deaf People

Hearing dogs' red jackets are specially designed to make them easy to spot in public places.

Dogs for the disabled

Assistance dogs live with people who have a physical disability or who have to use a wheelchair. These dogs can do lots of jobs for their owners. They can open doors, pick up dropped items, carry bags, and even switch lights on and off.

For a person in a wheelchair, everyday tasks can be very difficult. This dog is helping its owner get a box of cereal out of the kitchen cabinet.

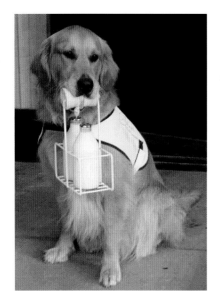

Many assistance dogs are "rescue" dogs. These are dogs that were once abandoned or badly treated by unkind people. Their new owners are glad to have them and take good care of them.

Activities

- What is your favorite kind of working dog? Why? Write about a day in that dog's life. Describe what it does.

- Look at these pictures of two dogs from the book. Which one is the police dog? What does the other dog do?

- Draw or paint a picture of your favorite working dog. Write a sentence about what the dog does underneath the picture.

- Choose a time for dog-spotting. During this time, make a note of any working dogs you see on the street, on television, or in books and magazines. What kind of dog did you spot most often?

Glossary

assistance dogs
type of dog that gives help to injured or disabled people

breed
type of dog such as a poodle or terrier

cattle
cows that are kept on a farm or ranch

criminals
people who have committed a crime and broken the law

herding
rounding up sheep or cattle and moving them somewhere new, such as a field

illegal
when something is against the law

natural disaster
a large accident or emergency caused by nature, such as an earthquake

partially sighted
when somebody cannot see very well

physical disability
a problem with part of your body that stops you from doing things

scent
special smell that only a dog can recognize

Index